"A new year begins. A man dies. A man who is strung out. Desperate. In need. Lost. A man most would quickly pass on the street, most avoiding contact, most looking the other way. In Sharon SingingMoon's remarkable book, *The Weight of One Hummingbird Feather,* readers are invited to meet this man and the ones who knew him, invited to see and feel what has been lost and what has been left behind with his passing. In this multifaceted journey of hurt, love and healing, SingingMoon's poetry soars, and we are privileged to be there to share and to witness."

> -Terry Allen, *Monsters in the Rain, Art Work, Waiting on the Last Train* and *Rubber Time*

"The best way to review Sharon SingingMoon's book, *The Weight of One Hummingbird Feather,* is by using her own words. Addiction, she states, "calls the tunes," and leaves loved ones behind with the "maybes" knowing full well that the deceased "was more/than the addiction that took him." In the end, she concludes that "hope clings/to frozen branches." Poignancy is learned experientially, sadly."

> -Nancy Jo Allen, *Wrinkles in Time and in Love* and *Wild and Tame.*

"Sharon SingingMoon's new poetry collection, *The Weight of One Hummingbird Feather* is a tragic memoir of the loss of her son to drug addiction in early January 2023. These raw and honest poems reveal not just her son's descent into addiction but also his healthy years of promise. Imagine a mother's pain witnessing her son's hopes and potential disintegrate overtime because of amphetamine, methamphetamine, and fentanyl use, which finally claimed his life. Imagine the pain his 8-year-old daughter felt when she found the body of her beloved daddy. The poems are powerful, raw and emotional. One cannot read them without empathy and compassion. SingingMoon not only shares her grief but also wants readers to learn about street drugs, such as fentanyl, which are taking countless lives today. She was helpless, unable to change her son's choices. Sharing the intimate details of the path his life took and her forever grief over the loss of her son takes courage. SingingMoon is a skilled poet, and I believe many parents will relate to these impactful poems."

-Barbara Harris Leonhard, *Three-Penny Memories, A Poetic Memoir.*

The Weight of One Hummingbird Feather

Poems by Sharon SingingMoon

Spartan
Press

Spartan Press

Kansas City, MO

spartanpresskc.com

Spartan
Press

First Edition: 1 3 5 7 9 10 8 6 4 2

ISBN: 978-1-958182-50-5

LCCN: 2023948181

Cover image: Sharon SingingMoon

Author photo: Agnes Vojta

Acknowledgments:

Deep gratitude to John Dorsey, former Poet Laureate of Belle Missouri for his talent & generosity; Walter Bargen, First Poet Laureate of Missouri for his knowledge & commitment to poetry; Inflections – Walter, Matt, Lois, Barb, Cami, Zak, Cortney & Lynne for their support, suggestions & comradery; Fourth Wednesday Critique Group – Barb, David, Joe, Melinda for sharing & for listening; the Columbia Chapter of the Missouri Writers Guild & the editors of Well Versed Anthology.

Many thanks to the editors of books & journals where these poems have appeared. "Micky's Purple Bike:" *Random Seed* (Compass Flower Press, 2018), "Overdose, January 2, 2023:" *Anti-Heroine Chic*, 2023, "Christmas Chaos:" *Anti-Heroine Chic*, 2023

TABLE OF CONTENTS

Where do the gone things go?

-Kimiko Hahn, from *In Childhood*

For every parent who loves an adult child who is addicted. These poems represent my experience with my son who died of an overdose on January 2, 2023. He was 46. He loved his daughter. She was 8 when she found his body on the floor.

Overdose January 2, 2023

he left us drowning
swimming in a raging sea
his love a needle

foil wrapped pills - unknown
origin – or a bottle
stolen from Breaktime

a year or two or more - no contact
then desperate calls
"send a ticket - bus or plane
it's raining, cold
in California
miss seeing you at Christmas
I'm tired
in jail in Indiana
in Tennessee
in Missouri
bail me out
I got beat up
my car was stolen
I'm OK
send money
can't wait to get back on the road"

he was a good playmate -
adulthood beyond his grasp -

he loved his daughter
made a cake for her eighth birthday

loved her but not enough to protect her
she found him on the floor
bloody from the face-first-fall
as he collapsed

did he know he was dying
somewhere between the high
& the falling
did he remember when he was young
& strong & filled with potential
before he chose the drugs
he thought set him free

Mixologists

in a trailer/lab somewhere
mixologists cook
ammonia hydroxide, battery acid,
drain cleaner, lantern fuel, antifreeze
with over-the-counter amphetamines
to produce methamphetamine
meth
mixed with fentanyl
methamphetamine & fentanyl
a speedball
you can smoke it
shoot it
light it up
inhale the fumes -
higher, lower – nowhere

One Feather

just 2 milligrams -
the weight of one hummingbird feather -
stops the breath
while those with deep pockets lie
knowing the true nature
of what they peddle
their dollars pile up
as thousands die

White Bread

A room of unmade beds, stained sheets
barely used for sleep
stagnant, dark
boundaries fluid
actions unaccounted for

The kitchen
encased in plastic
a laboratory
where toothless t-shirted men
sample poison dreams as they cook

Bottles of Mountain Dew close
a silent TV
rocks toddlers into dullness
their shit-filled diapers
pile up beside beer cans outside the door

In the yard
a calf of mysterious origin
appears at dawn
fenced with road crew orange
it cries for its teat

A school bus stops
near a no-name mailbox
a girl roughly dressed, hair matted, hesitant

stashes books in a five-gallon bucket
walks up the gravel road

She opens a door
to the smell of sweat
beer, tobacco
& chemicals
this is her home

She finds white bread
old bologna
cuts the sandwich into 4ths
sits between toddlers on a sagging couch
hands each a share

Her mother reeking with rage
back aching, teeth painful
staggers in from 10-hours at Git-n-Go
6-pack & smokes in hand
she tosses day-old roller-dogs toward the couch

The girl waits silent
becoming small, invisible
experience tells her nothing good can happen
in a trailer house in a field
on a dead-end gravel road

Unsheltered - October Tuesday

shelters empty out
camps along the hi-way, in neighboring woods
disband for the day
wanderers begin their solemn marches
a backpack, dirty blanket, shopping cart
maybe a trash bag of possessions

at designated intersections its shift work
they stand, wait for strangers' generosity
cardboard signs offer blessings
proclaim 'hungry', 'disabled vet'
some find a doorway, a lucky spot by a coffee shop
hopeful for a dropped coin, discarded butt

a woman, grey hair blowing
sits by a car that is also her bed, her closet
her home
plastic tubes run from her nose to a canister
near the crate that is her stool
her sign says 'anything helps'
but no one does

they're queued up twenty deep
at the plasma donation center
it pays $20 for their blood
$20 more if they bring a friend
gives out juice and a cookie after
so no one passes out

that's a solid offer, worth the wait
as Tuesday stretches out gray & wet

a soup kitchen serves up meager meals
doors open at 5, first come till it's gone
a shelter may have a cot

or that camp where someone scored cheap whiskey
to mask the weight of always waiting
for a hot meal, a dollar bill, a bed, sheet of plastic
some settle for a laugh, drunken stories, useful tips
& continue the wait for a kind word, a better option

Is This a Disease?

The street corner is alive with jokers & liars & drunks
talking shit, holding signs, camping in doorways
begging for dollars, stealing liquor
at 15 he sneaks out late
prefers the streets to his safe bed & hot meals

> a mother drives by at midnight
> hoping to find her missing one
> in the light of day the borrowed bike
> sits in an alley by a dumpster, tires gone

it is useless to wish when "fuck you"
was the final fling of words
aimed at the heart
anything to set him free
from accountability, responsibility
from the one he calls a bitch
the one who tries to save him
who pays the bondsman
always lets him back in

says nothing about the missing money
blankets, bikes, wine
the one who, hopeful, lends him a car - later
must explain when the police call -
the car found totaled by a downtown bar
abandoned

a mother cries

tries not to believe

this is who he chooses to be

The Leavings

a child – a puzzle – a person
we carry, birth, belong to each other
until we don't
we gather broken pieces
fit them together
what is missing
may be what is needed most

blinded by the day-to-day
we can only be who we are
maybe more/better tomorrow
excuses – reasons
we are persons
often brought to our knees
by this sacred task

in rooms with strangers
we bleed our sorrows, regrets
seeds planted
we take responsibility
for choices made by others

still we question
make an account of past failures
a balance sheet of wishes – chances
seek a way to regain control
over what we never really controlled

they walk out the door
bundled in their own dreams
leaving behind what pieces no longer fit
we sort through the detritus
wonder

A Slow Burn

Is it in the DNA - a genetic probability
a pastime erupting into need
a party that becomes a disease
an easy way out or in
drinking too much when you're fifteen
feels like the world is spinning
& you are free

by forty-six
it takes so much more
being the loudest
telling tales on the corner
for a hit, a snort, a shot
no longer enough
putting that needle in your body
is an intentional act
a desperate seeking
a casual disregard
for life

Christmas Chaos

We're happy to hear his voice on the phone
it's been another year of wondering, worrying
he says he wants to come home for Christmas
he needs a ticket
but first, he needs a copy of his birth certificate
to get a new ID
to pick up the ticket
then he needs to be picked up
at the airport 150 miles away
he arrives at 11 pm
he missed the original flight

There is no luggage
after living on the streets
all has been lost, discarded, traded, stolen
he needs to be treated for lice
the hair buried in the garden
someone takes him shopping for clothes
he asks for money to buy gifts
we've learned from the past
no money will be given

He yells that no one trusts him
he curses, calls a friend, slips out
is a no-show for Christmas Eve dinner
rolls in about noon on Christmas day

shaky, smelly, red-eyed
complains about left-overs
opens the hastily gathered gifts
asks for the receipts - just in case
we do not ask "where have you been?"
why spoil a perfect family gathering

Reports from the Road

Mom, I'm in jail
all I did was take a bottle from Breaktime
can you bail me out
I promise I'll show up for court
this time

Mom, we're getting kicked out
our utilities are shut off
we need to stay in your apartment – OK
I'm not getting a job so
Fuck you then

Mom, I need to come home
I'm tired
I have lice
they say Bob Marley
had twenty-seven kinds of lice in his dreads
when he died
send money – no
a bus ticket - OK

Mom, I'm in the hospital in Cali
I gave them your address
the guy warned me he is positive
Hep-C – I took the needle anyway
the test is positive
send a bus ticket – OK

Mom, I was hitching
I went to the bathroom
the guy took off with all my stuff
I'm in Waynesville
come pick me up

Mom, I'm in L.A.
I just got out of the hospital
I was sleeping in a parking garage
got attacked, beat up
I gave them your address for the bill
send money – no
Fuck you then

Mom, I'm in New Jersey
I met this girl at a show
we're living together
her dad wants to give me a job
I'm sitting alone in a parking lot
drinking – not sure why
she says she loves me

Mom, I need a copy of my birth certificate
send it to my buddy's address
I need an ID
I got pulled over - DWL
it's fucked up here in Georgia

Mom, I'm in jail in Indiana
you have to go find her

she's pregnant
drinking a lot
can you bail me out

Mom, I was at a show in Colorado
Red Rocks
dancing my ass off
they say I had a seizure
I'm OK now
staying with these kids I met
they have a car
send money – no
Fuck you then

All the Trimmings

after a year or more with no contact
you show up on Thanksgiving
a torn backpack, dreadlocks & expectations

a turkey dinner with all the trimmings
& no responsibility - but this year
my plans do not include cooking

weather perfect, I take you on a hike
let you ramble, glamorize life on the road
on the way back I buy you Taco Bell

offer some wine – you finish the bottle
tomorrow I'll take you to Goodwill for
new jeans & a couple of t-shirts

I wonder where you've really been
but don't ask – have said it all before
I save my tears for after you leave

Closing Time

a hand caresses
a tongue licks
tickles your ear
it's a stranger's kiss
you never knew you needed
breathy whispers
turn your head toward
a dead-end alley
lure you deeper
ride your back
lift you up
throw you down
stomp your face
strip you naked
fuck you raw
& when you rise to your knees
body screaming
throw away everything
for just one more time
you will know
not all demons dance
but they do call the tune

Push/Pull

You run

return

run again

even when you reach out

only your terms apply:

       1) Ask no questions

       2) Listen to your stories of the road

       3) Show appropriate amazement

       4) Give you what you ask for

       5) Expect nothing in return

Autopsy Report

body received in an unsealed black body pouch
clad in a gray t-shirt &
navy-blue lemon-printed pajama pants
red morgue ID tag around his left ankle

> he loved his baby sister
> slept on the floor by her crib
> "to catch her if she fell"
> taught her to call him Bubba

decedent found unresponsive on bedroom floor
pronounced dead at the scene
drug paraphernalia present
reported history of polysubstance use

> he used cruel words to escape our care
> ran from rehab, joked of prison
> we searched for why
> could not save him

toxicologic analysis of blood
positive findings: amphetamine,
methamphetamine, fentanyl

> who to blame, what to say
> when to tell his daughter
> addiction
> is true of the daddy who loved her

All the Broken Places

I open the box, the computer file
photographs document
the moments
he tried - was a good person
loved the family - himself
but not enough
chasing the next adventure
whatever it was
getting high
living on the streets
not all un-housed people are without
loved ones who miss them
wish them better
send help when asked
bail money
bus tickets, plane tickets
a place to live, rehab

Yard Boss

Sure, he did his duty with the hens, but really, he served
no other purpose. He ate too much, ran roughshod
over the yard, and intimidated the neighbor's dog who
was forced to lay on top of the doghouse watching
while his food was eaten. The neighbors complained so
- I had to kill the rooster.

My son, age ten, and his friend were recruited to catch
that brazen bird. They cornered the rooster, delivered
him to me and were impressed when I grabbed the
rooster's head, quickly swung him around, lay his
body on a stump and chopped. The hens, showing
no interest in the fate of their demanding yard-boss,
continued scratching.

Plucked, singed, in the pot, he was tough and stringy.
The dumplings were tasty.

Emboldened by their rooster- catching dexterity,
the boys huddled behind the outhouse whispering,
hatching a plot. I noticed their gathering supplies, but
was distracted by towels stuck in the wringer.

The screams got my attention. I ran around the house
to find hens flying, cackling madly. Boys, dressed
in swim goggles, fins, a snorkel, and garden gloves,
were laughing hysterically. His teen-aged sister was
screaming, batting away hens, and throwing a book at
them while covering her head with the blanket she had
been lying on.

After the excitement, we packed a lunch of egg salad sandwiches and spent the afternoon at the creek hunting for fossils. My son found a good trilobite and we found a couple of crinoids. His sister refused to eat as a protest against being threatened by goggle-wearing boys throwing chickens.

Micky's Purple Bike

Its summer and I'm off on my bike
in the cool morning breeze
I hear birds singing
in the maple trees

I may zip past the post office
or stop by the mill
or coast to the school house
and pedal hard up the hill

Then round the stop sign, turn right
and down the hill I fly
to the cottonwood tree
I wave to neighbors as I speed by

I stop at the old safe and the general store
just say, hello, maybe get a pop
then off to the big barn
so much to do, I just can't stop

I whiz through the air, wind in my face
I lean in on the fast curves
I feel free, I feel brave
I pedal strong with muscle and nerve

it's something I like
this power I give my purple bike

Somewhere in Indiana

1.

Somewhere in Indiana a young woman sits in the mud
waiting
she caresses a forty ounce malt liquor
a Bud Light chaser
close at hand
the seven-month fetus she carries
is shrunken, barely alive

her boyfriend
knows how
has hustled at the shows
been miracled in
was slanging whatever – she doesn't recall
but she was definitely high -
he was nailed - now he's in jail
for flipping on the lot - his Man
nowhere to be found

she's pranging out
the concert's over
it rained all night, campsites
abandoned, mud ankle-deep
she doesn't remember where their tent is
was that even their tent
or just an empty one

2.

the town square is lined with law offices
specializing in drug charges
for a set fee
parents can get their kids
out of jail
charge it over the phone

3.

she hears her name
tries to get up
stumbles, falls back on one elbow
gets to her knees, turns
a woman she thinks she knows
says "come with me"

finally coaxed
she follows
to the car
to a truck stop for food
a pregnancy test
- positive - she is skinny
pale, hair dirty
she is carrying the grandchild
I fear is already lost

4.

Wichita Kansas – Dr. Tiller
fetal alcohol syndrome
severe -

"if the fetus were to survive…
unlikely…." a late-term
termination an act of mercy

she is no longer pregnant
when she returns
to the parents who
would not go after her
who question
what about her scholarship
her future?

Past Perfect Tension

maybe if
I had not been working in that bar
tending to demands of daytime
drinkers
watching a truck driver
bite a bar glass
chew & swallow

maybe if
I had not worn that afro wig
he would not have ask me -
was it love or sex
desperation -
to move in
maybe
we would not have
gotten married
me pregnant

maybe if
my mother had not been depressed
had paid attention
had not spent her days chain smoking
reading Zane Grey over & over

maybe if
her father had not died

if her mother had stayed
she would not have felt abandoned

maybe if
she had noticed
my dad would have kept
his hands off me – and my cousin
maybe then I would not have been so
available

maybe if I had chosen
a better father for you
one who worked
did not hit or drink
or shoot coke & heroine
in the basement
behind the furnace

maybe if I had left sooner
not gone back that time

maybe if I had had
a different life
had been
a different person
maybe you would have been
different too

My Job?

was it my job to know everything you hid from me?

I didn't know you were sneaking out at fifteen
I didn't know you were stealing alcohol,
  getting drunk
  when you were sleeping with an older girl
  I begged her mother to send you home
    she wouldn't

I didn't know how many times you lied

  I wanted to trust you
  but you quit school
  packed your stuff –
  jeans, t-shirts
  the new shoes -
    left town with that girl

I didn't know where you were
how could I know until you called
collect from a jail somewhere

  I wanted to save you
  I tried – drove all night more than
  once or twice
  slept in cheap motels with
  questionable sheets
  to rescue you from yourself
    from the streets

I begged you, fought for you
paid for counseling
with borrowed money
gave you an apartment
took you to the ER, to rehab

you wouldn't stay
you took & took & left
        again & again you ran away
screaming stinging words
a trash bag of stuff over one shoulder
until you said meth & heroine –
I didn't know how far
you had fallen

Principles of EFFECTIVE TREATMENT
from the National Institute on Drug Abuse – US NIH

Research shows that when treating addictions to opioids
(prescription pain relievers or drugs like heroin or
fentanyl), medication should be the first line of treatment,
usually combined **with** some form of behavioral therapy
or counseling. Medications are also available to help treat
addiction to alcohol and nicotine.

Additionally, medications are used to help people detoxify
from drugs, although detoxification is not **the** same as
treatment and is not sufficient to help a **person** recover.
Detoxification **al**one **wi**thout subsequent treatment
generally leads **to** resumption of drug use.

For people with addictions to drugs like stimulants or
cannabis, no medications are currently available to assist
in treatment, so treatment consists of behavioral therapies.
Treatment should be tailored to address each patient's
drug use patterns and drug-related medical, mental, and
social problems.

Discoveries in science lead to breakthroughs in drug use
treatment.

What medications and devices help TREAT DRUG
ADDICTION?

Different types of medications and devices may be useful
at different stages of treatment to help a patient **stop
using drugs**, stay in treatment, and avoid **relapse**.

• Treating withdrawal. When patients first stop using drugs, they can experience various physical and emotional symptoms, including restlessness or sleeplessness, as well as depression, anxiety, and other mental health conditions. **Certain** treatment...

Storms on the Horizon

We sat on the porch - watched
black clouds, flashes of lightening
heard rumbling thunder
grow louder as storms rolled across

Chores could wait as we breathed in
cool air coming with the rain

When your child is six or eight
you brush aside the signs
parental love will not allow
the naming of concerns
fear of a coming storm

When I visited in northern California
he spoke of how the storms
are not as beautiful as the storms we watched
from our porch in Missouri

That childhood in a tiny town - a garden
a kitten, chickens & a wood stove
was a gift - a memory he held on to
even as he let go so much

Gandhi Was a Hero

I see him standing on the seat of his bike
coasting down Main Street
fearless – Mom, look at me –
I yell encouragement
he named his kitten Kitty Pretty
chased the chickens
hated stacking wood

was voted 'best dressed boy' in sixth grade
second-hand parachute pants
the collar popped on his Izod polo
it mattered to him then
what brand the sneakers, how he looked

he bought a rose for the girl
their first date
too young to drive
they met at the theatre
he was handsome with a fresh hair cut
nervous

in junior high he won the debate
"yes, Gandhi was a hero
greater than any sports figure"
his charisma carried them

a knock on my door at 1 am
his best friend's father asking
where are they?

sneaking out at night
the beginning of it

I give his daughter
"the first book your daddy ever read by himself"
she loves him
says she knows he is up in heaven

now I sit in the crematorium
filling out forms
how to say I fought for him
remember he was more
than the addiction that took him

Not all Ever-afters end Happily

hope clings
frozen to branches
family – the extended & the disengaged
seek warm hugs
in snow-packed gatherings
thaw then freeze up again
in the space between
there is ice enough for gin & tonics
only some will drink
others cast about for
more, better, stronger
we notice, worry –
hope

The Loss of You

We tried to save you in the name of love
fought with you/for you because of our love

Traumatized to find you dead on the floor
when fatherhood seemed to fit like a glove

Your young daughter is left fatherless now
she imagines you in heaven above

I search old photos – see your shining face
recall your joy in the life you once loved

I write poems, rage at the loss of you
alone with drugs, what were you thinking of

An urn of the ashes that once were you
now sits on the shelf in a dark alcove

Wild stories told in the kitchen no more
now it's the sad coo of a mourning dove

You'll never know your daughter - a woman
graduate, married - a mother who loves

Alone in a room I sort through your stuff
t-shirts & movies, an old baseball glove

Tears flow for the boy – the potential lost
moon singing in the night shines from above

Drawn to the Sweetness

a juvenile hummingbird
last of the season
circles the feeder
chases away the bees
drawn to the sweetness

ants who climbed the witch hazel
found their way into the feeder
seeking a sugar high
now float dead
in the sweetness they craved

More Reports from the Road

Mom, these meth-heads
attacked me
I wasn't even talking to them
send a ticket
I'm in San Fran – I lost my ID

Mom, I'm in a Tennessee jail
just for selling on the lot at a show
I was miracled in
the public defender says
18 months is a good deal

Collect call from a Tennessee Correctional Facility
Do you accept the charges - yes
Mom, calling from prison in Tennessee
I hang with the Mexicans
the Black dudes are too scary
the skinheads are too
guess what, I read a book – a whole book
it's boring here

Collect call from a Tennessee Correctional Facility
Do you accept the charges - yes
Mom, guess what
I got my GED
I go to class because it's so boring here
I might get out on work release
but I have to come back every night
that sucks

Mom, I'm in Arcadia Cali
I made a bunch of money trimming pot
went to town
had a steak dinner got a little drunk
bought a blanket from some street kids
rolled up next to some house, passed out
when I woke up
all my cash was gone
I guess that means
I'm not supposed to have money

Mom, she's pregnant
I'm gonna be a dad
we're getting an apartment here in Cali
come for Thanksgiving - OK

Mom, send money
I need to get a lawyer
she's trying to take my kid
send money – no
Fuck you then

Year of the Dragon

Born in the Year of the Dragon
the sign of Aquarius
on Valentine's Day
over-dosed in the winter
Year of the Tiger
under Capricorn
an inauspicious day
still
a mother's pain goes on & on
after the death of her child
she searches for a reason
hoping for something
knowing there was nothing

When news of your overdose death went 'round

1.
he was in the driveway when I got home
one of your friends from back then
he asked for a photograph

maybe some kids would get together
a celebration of you

he needed to share a memory
of when you were here for your sister's wedding

how he was the one you called
from the ER where I had taken you

withdrawal cramps & shakes were strong
he hooked you up - seemed proud to have helped

2.
another from your past called
expressing regret at the loss of a friend

said he is no longer into drugs
has taken methadone every day
for ten years

3.
he had stories, she said
was known as Mountain on the road
had adventures & what he called freedom

he told it again & again
how someone he knew
knew someone who told him

someone was *flying a flag* "God Bless"
this guy pulls up
hands him a hundred

word on the street
it could happen anytime
"made fifty in one day once"

we would score a room
some cheap place - if someone had an ID
fifteen kids on the floor, piled in beds

he made the road sound great
bragged about the shows
how to be *miracled in*

make money on the lot
get free drugs
talked as if prison was boring -
upped his street cred with BS
only brought his troubles home to Mom

But Not Today

Some days may need a push
just a little
to stop counting
wrongs, pains, tears
    do one thing
coffee, walk in the garden
breathe, touch something alive
smile intentionally
until smiling just happens
hang the wash
    feel, welcome the breeze
don't let the mind interfere
pick late tomatoes
cook them into a sauce
beautiful & thick
fill jars
boil until the lids pop
    remember winter
bake bread
make the bed
    do something useful
speak aloud & gently
to your heart
acknowledge small joys
    move slowly
keep moving
soon but not today
heartbreak
will soften into sweet memories

I Always Feared – Coda 1

I listen to the salesman
have already decided
but he is gentle – a distraction
his pitch caring & calm
well practiced

Papers are produced
signed – I am your closest relative
though I feel thousands of miles from where
how you ended up

I never pictured me
sitting with your ex-girlfriend
mother of your only child
filling out forms at a crematorium

Glass cases hold various products
to preserve memories
they will mail your remains
in a plastic bag, in a box

She chooses an urn
something to hold the ashes
that once were you
a charm for your daughter

I always feared it would end this way
body tired, mind confused
years of life on the streets

still I hoped you would grow exhausted
give it up – and now you have - accidentally

In the car she talks of how you lied
told her you were trying
doesn't mention her own
recent DUI

But that is not the point now
there must have been love
or what passed as love
between her & you
once upon a time

Do I miss you - Coda 2

The person you became
maybe not so much – it's a hard truth
for a parent to admit
you were gone so long
edges sharper, rougher
more prickly & defensive
each time you returned
reeking with anger
tossing cruelty like candy at a parade
you needed to preserve the identity you crafted
the glory of the road
only called when you needed to be rescued
from the consequence of your choices

you could never keep a cell phone
we could never contact you
just to know you were alive
we feared you would die
a John Doe
somewhere along a hi-way
or in a camp of unhoused
in a graveyard you said
was a safe place for sleeping
in a parking garage where strangers beat you

I do not miss the worry
the fights when you came 'round
your calls from a jail in another state
begging for help

a ticket, money
the bondsmen harassing me to pay
when you skipped out again

I remember your laugh
the crazy card game you
tried to teach us
that time you showed up for Christmas
how you helped build the arbor
for the wild wisteria
we could never get it plumb
but it's still standing
a reminder that you could be OK
even kind
that we could have fun together

the potential - the possibility
you would recover
heal the wounds

I do miss believing that
being a dad would be enough
that you would finally grow
weary of the road
of the drugs

I miss the hope

Dylan Thomas Michael Battley (Mountain)
02-14-1976 – 01-02-2023

Notes:

I sourced the eraser poem from a page of the National Institutes of Health (NIH) - National Institutes on Drug Abuse. The poems, *Reports from the Road* & *More Reports from the Road*, are actual calls received from my son over the course of his years of addiction & his travels from one situation to another. The poem, *The Loss of You* is a Ghazal, an Arabic poetic form.

George Richard Tiller, M.D. (August 8, 1941 – May 31, 2009) an American physician from Wichita, Kansas, the medical director of Women's Health Care Services, one of only three clinics nationwide at the time which provided late term termination of pregnancy. Tiller was frequently targeted with protests and violence by anti-abortion groups and individuals. His clinic was firebombed in 1986. In 1993 Tiller was shot in both arms by an anti-abortion extremist. On May 31, 2009, while serving as usher at his church, Tiller was fatally shot in the side of the head by an anti-abortion extremist.

According to the US DEA, Fentanyl is a potent synthetic opioid drug first synthesized in Belgium by Paul Janssen under the label of his newly formed Janssen Pharmaceutical in 1959. Janssen Pharmaceutical is now a division of Johnson & Johnson. Fentanyl was approved by the US FDA for use as an analgesic (pain relief) and anesthetic. It is also used as a large animal sedative. Fentanyl is approximately 100 times more potent than morphine and 50 times more potent than heroin as an analgesic. On the street, Fentanyl is known as *China Town, Dance Fever,*

Friend, King Ivory, Murder 8, Poison, and by other names. Fentanyl is snorted, smoked, taken orally by pill or tablet, spiked onto blotter paper, patches, sold alone or mixed with heroin and other substances, has been identified in fake pills, mimicking pharmaceutical drugs such as oxycodone.

"I was trying to not let in the tears over Sharon's poetry. It reminded me of [ ] who is an addict and what [ ] goes through with him. To channel it the way she did was so profound"

-HDI

Sharon SingingMoon is a poet & award-winning visual artist living in mid-Missouri. She draws inspiration from the natural world & our human struggle to balance mind/body/spirit in the face of our own hubris. In between long hikes she dabbles in screen writing & is working on a YA historical fiction novel. Sharon has a Master's in Public Administration & worked as a lobbyist for social justice, spearheading several progressive advances in Missouri. Sharon's writing has appeared in *Interpretations*, several volumes of *Well Versed anthology*, *Anti-Heroin Chic*, *Masticadores USA*, *Silver Birch Press* & others. Her non-fiction piece, *The Honey Tree*, took first place among non-fiction submissions to *Well Versed* 2023. Her previous poetry collection, *Random Seed*, as well as this new collection, can be found at independent bookshops across the mid-west, at Barnes & Nobel & on Amazon.

This project was made possible, in part, by generous support from the Osage Arts Community.

Osage Arts Community provides temporary time, space and support for the creation of new artistic works in a retreat format, serving creative people of all kinds — visual artists, composers, poets, fiction and nonfiction writers. Located on a 152-acre farm in an isolated rural mountainside setting in Central Missouri and bordered by ¾ of a mile of the Gasconade River, OAC provides residencies to those working alone, as well as welcoming collaborative teams, offering living space and workspace in a country environment to emerging and mid-career artists. For more information, visit us at www.osageac.org

Osage Arts Community